ALONG THE TRAIL

A Photographic Essay of Glacier National Park
and the Northern Rocky Mountains

ALONG THE TRAIL

A Photographic Essay of Glacier National Park
and the Northern Rocky Mountains

Photographs by Danny On

Text by David Sumner

Published by the Glacier Natural History Association, Inc.
in cooperation with The Lowell Press, Kansas City, Missouri

Many persons were responsible for this book. The book was first conceived by the Board of Directors of the Glacier Natural History Association, Inc.; the family and friends of the late Danny On; and the staffs of Glacier National Park, the Flathead National Forest and the National Bison Range.

Special encouragement was given by the chairman of the board of directors of the association, Chet Ellingson; Glacier National Park Superintendent Phillip R. Iversen and his staff. Project coordinator was Edwin L. Rothfuss, Superintendent of Mt. Rushmore National Memorial and formerly executive secretary of the association.

Others whose talent and energy helped bring the book to completion were Payson W. Lowell, president of The Lowell Press; Barbara W. Funk, editor; David E. Spaw, designer; and members of the staff of The Lowell Press.

Library of Congress Cataloging in Publication Data
On, Danny.
Along the trail.
Published in cooperation with The Lowell Press, Kansas City, Mo.
1. Glacier National Park—Pictorial works.
I. Sumner, David.   II. Title.
F737.G5O6   779'.9'9178652   79-53223
ISBN 0-913504-53-X (Lowell)
ISBN 0-913504-54-8 (Lowell) pbk.

THIRD PRINTING
Printed in the United States of America
by The Lowell Press, Inc.

Dedicated to Danny On

TABLE OF CONTENTS

viii

In the mountains, the upbeat
glacier lily (Erythronium
grandiflorum) rushes spring.
Often it sprouts and blooms
within days after old winter
snowbanks melt from a site.
Sometimes it doesn't bother to
wait. In the northern Rockies
summer is brief.

FOREWORD

Danny On, University of Montana forestry graduate and Flathead National Forest silviculturist, perished January 21, 1979, in a skiing accident.

He was fifty-four years old, a native of Red Bluff, California, an Eagle Scout and a World War II paratrooper who served in the historic Battle of the Bulge and was wounded in action.

Among us are a few men and women who become legends even as they are friends and neighbors. Danny was such a man.

Danny On was known for his generosity, intelligence, respect for people and love of the outdoors. He lived and skied on Big Mountain and much enjoyed Glacier National Park. His photography also took him to the National Bison Range, Bob Marshall Wilderness, the Canadian parks and Alaska.

John Emerson, Flathead National Forest supervisor, was a college classmate of Danny at the University of Montana from 1946 to 1951. Emerson recalled: "Danny was expert in everything that I knew he did, whether it be as a skier, silviculturist or photographer. He was a competent professional. He easily made friends wherever he went. His manner was to please people. From my knowledge of going to school and working with him, I don't know of anyone who said anything against Danny."

Glacier National Park Superintendent Phil Iversen commented on Danny On's love of the park's natural beauty. "He seemed to absorb the tranquility that exists in the park. In his quiet way, he touched each of us while the noisy clamored for attention."

A memorial service was held January 27, 1979, with more than three hundred friends attending. At times, voices wa-

Photo of Danny On: Jon Cates

vered with emotion as professional associates, friends and family paid tribute.

Dr. Les Pengelly, wildlife biologist at the University of Montana, noted: "Danny had immortalized the outdoors with his photography, and the many appearances he had made with his slides. All assembled here have had our lives shaped by Danny. He probably would have been embarrassed by all this attention. Instead, he would have suggested, 'Let's head for the hills.' "

This retired editor of the *Hungry Horse News* is among the people who received brief letters signed "Your friend, Danny." All of us knew what Les Pengelly meant when he said, "That could have been signed, 'Everyone's friend, Danny.' "

This unassuming forester became Montana's best-known wildlife photographer. His death on January 21, 1979, was a shock. A reaction was the desire expressed by friends and admirers that there should be a book to treasure of Danny On photographs.

Danny On was a long-time member of the board of the Glacier Natural History Association, a non-profit organization whose net proceeds are used to further such efforts as conservation education.

Glacier Natural History Association arranged with Danny On's brothers and

sisters to have use of his photographs, and the first product of the arrangement is this book.

Mel Ruder
Editor emeritus, *Hungry Horse News*
Columbia Falls, Montana

ALONG THE TRAIL

A Photographic Essay of Glacier National Park
and the Northern Rocky Mountains

PRAIRIE

As if they sensed their words would otherwise fall short, those who have described the American prairie have instinctively reached toward poetry.

"The land is in the shape of a ball...inland sea.... The land is almost as big as the sky above . . . grassland sea . . . waves of grass. . . . Elsewhere the sky is the roof of the world, but here the earth was the floor of the sky."

Whatever the phrase, the unspoken suggestion was the same. As an expanse of land, the prairie was so excessively spacious it was disorienting. The relief dipped and swelled, but basically there was nothing to stop the eye until the horizon. That was merely the end of what you could see, and beyond you knew there was more of the same. Lines on the prairie were straight, or quietly curving—merging to vanishing points at the end of sight. Always there was something drawing you on.

As Europeans settled America, one landscape after another awed them. Forest and swamp seemed impenetrably dark, mountains grand and unclimbable, rivers roads to anywhere. But none struck the eye like the prairie. None stirred such a sense of openness, plenty, possibility or space.

From Montana's Bob Marshall Wilderness north to Canada's great national parks, Jasper and Banff, prairie laps against the Rockies both east and west. On the east the vastness is greater: a huge, rolling space running all the way back to Minnesota and Manitoba before trees wall up to stop it. On the west there are only pockets: broad valleys and broader basins where the apparent emptiness of the land is its preponderant fact. Western Montana is honeycombed with such spots: the National Bison Range at Moiese, the Flathead Valley, the Big Hole country and the Bowdoin National Wildlife Refuge.

Prairie emptiness is, of course, a deception, a trick on the eye by space. Dominant facts of the prairie world are vivid, few and strong. First is dryness, sometimes extending to drought. Next is constant wind, then low relief, next fine soils which blow away when not held in place by growth, and finally temperature extremes. On the northern plains, daytime August heat can hold near 100°F for weeks; February cold can sink to –40°F with the wind adding a chill factor that doubles the drop.

There are occasional exceptions. Rivers and creeks flow across the prairie. Some water lush, improbable valleys; others cut canyons, and many are lined with trees—cottonwoods, alders, willows. Occasionally too, the prairie blisters upward to foothill islands thatched in aspen, ponderosa pine and Douglas fir. But such exceptions need be noted only so they can be dropped. The overriding character of the prairie is what conditions its life.

It is a life of adaptation to sharp limits. Of all plants, grasses define the prairie like none other. Against the Rockies, shortgrasses predominate, though in wet years, or when grazing is light, midgrasses may abound as well. It is easy to overlook these grasses and their evolved suitability to prairie life. They are common, produce no showy flowers and to the untrained eye appear monotonously alike. But both their variety and ingenuity are apt.

By design, grasses are pollinated not by insects but by wind, one of the most dependable facts of the prairie. Seedlings rush into growth—sinking primary roots to precious water in as little as three days. Unlike those of most trees and shrubs, grass leaves grow not from the tips but from the base so that grazing—be it by bison, grasshopper or cow—does not destroy these plants. Grass roots are so fibrous and minute that a single square yard may hold twenty miles of them; the effect is to hold both soil and moisture.

Elsewhere on the prairie, the story is the same. Broad-leaved plants are numerous, and a feature of many is the capacity of their seeds to go dormant in drought cycles. During these same periods, deep-rooted perennials conserve water by cutting back on leaf production.

Many animal adaptations are responses to space and the absence of cover. Shelter for the bison was a thick, shaggy coat; defense was speed, strength and numbers. Pronghorns evolved even greater speed, endurance and eight-power eyes. Prairie dogs also have sharp eyes plus burrowing skill, community and a quick, elaborate system of "barks" and chirps for warning fellows of approaching predators.

Of all the life zones of the northern Rockies, the prairie is today most altered—this because it is most useful and accessible. Beginning in the late 1860s, America discovered that its prairie grew "gold from the grass roots up" in the form of graze, and sent huge herds of cattle over the land, often destroying what they sought by overgrazing.

In a similar way, adaptations that served animals well when the prairie was wild keyed their destruction when it was tamed. The bison's herding instinct was apt defense against wolves, but fatal *en masse* when these animals were faced with men firing guns. Barbed wire mocked the antelope's speed. Community served prairie dogs well when coyotes approached, but hastened death when man scattered poisoned grain.

The American bison (Bison bison) is the largest North American land mammal. A mature, heavy-shouldered bull can weigh in near 3,000 pounds, stand more than six feet tall and measure over eleven feet from nose to rump. Before the white man, bison surged over the prairie in vast oceans of brown—sometimes over four million animals to a herd, covering an area twenty by fifty miles. The herding instinct evolved as a defense against predators, especially the wolf, but it also sped the bison's downfall because they refused to scatter and could be shot down in great numbers. By 1920, only twenty wild bison were known—down from sixty million animals in the early 1800s.

6

Discovered from a distance on the plain, a group of prong-horns (Antilocapra americana) will appear calm, though they've already fixed you with their eight-power eyes. Approach too close, and the whole herd will bolt and accelerate in unison, then flow swiftly across the prairie to a distant land swell where they'll slow and walk out of sight, watching you carefully as they go. Group alertness gives strength in numbers, but sometimes bucks become solitary as has this handsome, unusually tall-horned animal.

The life of a prairie cone-flower (Ratibida columnifera) may span fifty years, its story an open book on the steady change and wide extremes of the prairie world. In a dry year a plant may grow a few stalks, some rumpled leaves and no bloom at all. Come wet season, the same plant may produce ten stalks up to two feet tall, each one topped with a flower. Other years, grasshoppers or cattle may feed on it almost to the ground. Nothing static about the life of this plant.

The killdeer (Charadrius vociferus vociferus), left, is a shrill, jittery bird. Approach a killdeer nest, and the attending adult will make a high din while fluttering and flopping over the ground to decoy you away. This bird's odd name comes from its "kill-dee" call.

Purple prairie clover (Petalos-temon purpurem) grows east of the Great Divide only.

You can make a blue dye from the seeds of the prairie sun-flower (Helianthus petiolaris).

Flowers of the composite (Com-positae) family are among the most numerous in the Rockies.

A genuine, wild robin (Turdus migratorius propinquus) makes its suburban lawn cousin appear stolid and pale. Wild robins are shier, quicker to call warning and take flight.

A fleeting flash of color is all you normally see of the Western tanager (Piranga ludoviciana). The bright males are shy; the drab, olive-yellow females melt into the trees.

The great horned owl (Bubo virginianus) has an easily recognized and imitated call: a resonant, measured "whoo . . . whowho . . . whoo . . . whoo" with equal accent on each.

The fiercely territorial rufous hummingbird (Selasphorus rufus) defends its food sources by diving and buzzing at intruders. This is a female; males have glistening red throats.

The osprey (Pandion haliaetus) is sometimes called the "fish hawk" because it feeds entirely on fish. Above streams and rivers, it will hover in the air before dropping to the water like a shot, talons outstretched, after a catch. The osprey flies with a crook in its wings; it is dark above, white below and has a distinctive dark line through its eyes.

Always alert, seven prong-horns face all points of the compass, checking for danger. Pronghorns sleep only in short snatches, never deeply.

The mountain lion (Felis concolor) is solitary and often circles a territory sixty miles across in search of its main prey, the mule deer, which it hunts along wooded prairie streams and breaks where there is cover for stalking. With rare exceptions, antelope are too fast for the lion.

*An ecotone is an interface be-
tween different plant communities, richer in life because of
the mixing of worlds. At
lower St. Mary Lake, left, in
Glacier, the high prairie community fades into the forest
and growth becomes suddenly*

*more diverse. Yellow owl
clover (Orthocarpus luteus), a
late-blooming flower of the dry
foothill meadows, is among
many that appear as you hike
from the prairie to the first
tier of the mountain forests.*

Basking in late summer sun, these five painted turtles (Chrysemys belli) have an evolutionary ancestry dating back more than 200 million years. They feed on aquatic plants and insects.

With both right eye and ear pivoted toward the camera, this mountain cottontail (Sylvilagus nuttalli) is poised to bolt for cover.

In tense, lookout posture, the Columbian ground squirrel (Citellus columbianus) will signal danger to its fellows with a loud chirping.

FOREST

In the mountains, life is arranged in tiers. In the northern Rockies these number five—beginning with the high, rolling prairie which extends upward to between 3,000 and 4,500 feet and topping out with the austere alpine tundra which takes over between 5,500 and 8,000 feet.

Sandwiched between these extremes are the three great forest zones of the mountains: the transition (or foothills), the Canadian (or montane) and the Hudsonian (or subalpine). The designations are meant to be roughly comparative. A hike covering one thousand vertical feet in the mountains takes one through climactic and environmental changes similar to those he'd encounter on a six-hundred-mile northward trek.

In the foothills zone, growth is akin to that of the central United States; summers are warm and dry, winters cool and snowy, and the combination supports an ample array of trees and flowers. The montane zone parallels the tall forests of the northern United States and southern Canada. Summers are cool, winters cold, and snowcover the rule from November to May. The more severe the conditions, the less room for biologic luxuriance or error; life in the montane zone is drawn with greater economy than that of the foothills below. The subalpine is the uppermost forest zone, and like that of the region abutting Hudson's Bay. Summer days can be pleasant, but nights are chill and frost possible any time. Here life begins to show adaptations that are intensely opportunist and defensive both in response to increasingly severe conditions.

In aggregate, the terms of life in all these zones are markedly different than those down on the prairie. In contrast to the openness and exposure below, the mountain forests are closed in and sheltering. Whereas prairie plant life hunkers low out of the wind and dives deep for subsurface water, the dominant posture in the forests is a reaching upward. Here light, not water, is the ingredient in shortest supply; trees jostle, elbow and shove at each other to find sun.

Water, however, remains a persuasive factor, accounting for distinctly different forests east and west of the Great Divide. More dramatically in Glacier and Waterton National parks than in most

20

A western larch (Larix occidentalis) cone becomes its own intricate design. Like many trees of Glacier's western slope, the range of this larch extends from the Great Divide west to the Pacific, underscoring the wet northwestern quality of these forests. Western larches produce huge quantities of seeds and are often the first trees to grow back into an area hit by a forest fire.

reaches of the Rocky Mountain chain, the high rib of peaks draws most of the moisture from the clouds before they pass out over the eastern slope. At 4,500 feet on the west side of Glacier, a hike can readily take one into a dense, damp, verdant forest. At the same elevation on the east, he would wander the uppermost margin of the dry prairie.

The overall result of these multiple differences in elevation and moisture is to create a near crazy quilt of forest types within an unusually tight area. For example, most trees of the McDonald Valley on the west side of Glacier are the same that grow in the Pacific Coast ranges. Those on the east slope of the park are what one also finds in central Colorado.

These forests of the northern Rockies are its most forgiving environment. Life here is more abundant and diverse than on either the prairie below or the tundra above, and its mass is greater—all primarily because of more water, and the options it allows. Shelter and secluded space are everywhere—be it for birds to nest, for elk to calve or for grizzly bears to dig roots, den up, or avoid man.

Except where they have been timbered or cleared for development, the forests of the northern Rockies are less altered than its prairie. This hardly means they are static, for a forest, like all plant communities, is always in a kind of motion called succession. This process is not cyclical like seasonal or daily rounds; it does tend to recur, but usually over periods of hundreds, sometimes thousands of years.

The trigger that starts a forest succession may be an avalanche, a flood, a forest fire, a volcanic blast—anything that inflicts drastic change on an area right down to destruction of all its life. Not only does nature abhor such a vacuum; it strives to fill it with a community of life rightly suited to the climate and physical conditions of the place. That balance, or fullness, is known as climax; getting there is the process of succession.

Forest fires are the most vivid disasters to occur regularly in the forests of the northern Rockies. Directly afterward, all is devastation, but by the following spring, new growth usually begins to move in. These are the pioneers, the beginners of forest succession, most often leafy meadow flowers, herbs and low shrubs.

This, however, is just the beginning. West of the divide, lodgepole pines are likely to move in, grow and eventually shade out the meadow growth. Thus, in fifty or so years, another stage of succession has taken over: a virtual stockade of straight, skinny pines. Once again, this cannot last; lodgepoles do not reseed in their own shade, but Engelmann spruce and subalpine fir can. As the lodgepole forest ages, dies and falls, another successional stage is there—another forest growing up.

Where it grows, west of the divide in the northern Rockies, the spruce-fir community is the climax, the ideal growth for its site. As one generation of these trees ages and dies, young of the same species grow up and replace them. Always the forest is in process, always new life succeeding the old.

Each spring, female Canada geese (Branta canadensis) lay from four to eight large white eggs. Thirty days later they all hatch within a single day. Goslings may stay on the nest one more day before following their parents to water. They stay with their parents for one migration to learn the routes and seasonal homes. Then they're on their own.

Great blue herons (Ardea herodias) nest in treetop colonies along larger lakes and streams, feeding on fish, frogs and salamanders. They always fly with their necks folded back on their shoulders—never stretched out.

Slender of build and artful in its markings, the pintail (Anas acuta) pair up in the winter. Come spring, the drake follows the hen to her nesting ground, no matter where he was born or where he summered before.

Endangered species need not become extinct; the trumpeter swan (Olor buccinator) is proof. By the 1930s, drained marshes and hunting had reduced them drastically; now protected, they are up over 3,000.

The most abundant of wild ducks—the robin of waterfowldom—the mallard (Anas platyrhynchos), turns up just about everywhere there's open water and a little space. He is the ancestor of the domestic, barnyard duck.

West of the Divide the forest takes over at lower elevations than it does to the east. This is mainly because rainfall is greater west of the mountains. At 3,154 feet, Lake McDonald on the west side of Glacier National Park is well into the forested zone. Were it over the mountains to the east, it would be surrounded by waves of prairie grass.

Largest of all deer, the moose (*Alces alces*) is a loner and with good reason. Place a herd of moose in a limited area, and they'd soon strip it bare and face starvation. In winter, one moose needs about thirty pounds of browse daily just to live. Moose calves stay with their mothers only a year. Just before giving birth to a new calf, a cow will drive off its yearling—forcing it to seek a new range and keeping the population scattered and healthy. In Glacier, the North Fork of the Flathead River is prime moose habitat.

In summer, moose take to shallow forest ponds and bogs to escape heat and insects and also to feed. In the northern Rockies, yellow pond lilies (Nuphar polysepalum) and buckbean (Menyanthes trifoliata), below, are common fare in the most varied diet in the deer family.

The more forest fires, the more moose. The bulk of their diet consists of the meadow flowers, herbs, shrubs and leafy trees that sprout and thrive soon after a blaze. In contrast, moose food in old, dense conifer forests is near nil. When pines, spruce and fir move back into a burned area, as inevitably they do, the moose move out. Populations tumble until a new wave of fires restarts the cycle.

The peaks of the Canadian Rockies are higher than those south in Glacier; as a group they also tend toward greater sheer power and mass. The Icefields Parkway, which connects Banff and Jasper National Parks in Alberta, gives a majestic, unbroken, 142-mile panorama of these mountains, as well as of the glaciers that are carving them still today. The view, right, is across Bow Lake in Banff to Bow Peak (9,409 feet) in the center and Crowfoot Mountain (10,000 feet) to the far right. Globe huckleberry (Eaccinium globulare) bushes cover the near meadow, foreground and left; bears and birds and men all relish the tasty berries of this abundant, low shrub.

Beargrass (Xerophylum tenax) is a striking flower with many stories to tell. A member of the lily family, it blooms only once every four to seven years; thus, some years beargrass is profuse, while others it is sparse. Plants three feet tall are common. In winter, mountain goats graze beargrass's thin, wiry leaves. Indians of the northern Rockies dry and bleach the same leaves and weave baskets from them.

Queencups (Clintonia uni-
flora) prefer wet, wooded sites.

Indian paintbrush (Castelleja
sp.) is a semiparasite.

In lore, St. Johnswort (Hyperi-
cum formosum) expelled witches.

Blue-eyed grass (Sisyrinchium
angustifolium) is a tiny iris.

Like the prow of a sinking ship, right, Mt. Oberlin (8,180 feet) rides above the valleys leading away from Logan Pass in Glacier. To its right, Bird Woman Falls drops from the lip of a hanging valley. Implausible as it sounds, all the high peaks of the park are made of stacks of ancient seabeds and plains layered gradually for something exceeding a billion years. A mere 70 million years ago, these strata were forced upward, and just yesterday, in geologic time, glaciers carved them to their present relief.

35

Bog cranberries (Vaccinium vitis) are red, shiny and tart.

Butter-and-eggs (Linaria vulgaris) is a European import.

Fairyslipper orchids (Calypso bulbosa) bloom in small colonies in well shaded woods.

Silky phacelia (Phacelia sericea) is common along trails between 4,500 and 5,500 feet.

Dwarf huckleberries (Vaccinium caespitosum) are edible.

Smooth asters (Aster levis)
bloom until autumn frosts.

Serviceberry (Amelanchier
aln.) is vital mule deer browse.

Prince's pine (Chimaphila um-
bellata) has medicinal roots.

The mountain lady slipper (Cypripedium montanum) is among the rarest of orchids in the northern Rockies. As with most of this beautiful family, digging and trying to transplant this flower kills it because it is so finely attuned to its wild environment. Most orchids live in delicate balance with microscopic fungi. Others have little or no chlorophyll and must depend for food on certain kinds of decayed plant material. Still others can be pollinated only by a single species of insect. For all this family, life is specialized, and change means death.

Near timberline in midsummer, large yellow
monkeyflowers (Mimulus tilingii) splash
runnels of bright color down moist meadows
and along streams like water itself.

These slight blossoms belong to a substantial
shrub, mountainspray (Holodiscus discolor),
which often grows five feet tall. Unlikely as it
appears, this plant belongs to the rose family.

The Lewis and Clark expedition discovered
the Lewis monkeyflower (Mimulus lewisii)
while crossing the northern Rockies in 1805
when much of the region was part of the
newly purchased Louisiana Territory.

Cushion phlox (Phlox pulvinata) grows in a
classic alpine design. Hunched in a tight, low
mat, it avoids the whipping tundra winds,
conserves energy and reduces evaporation in
the dry, thin, high mountain air.

A cushion plant of the dry, exposed foothills, mountain Douglasia (Douglasia montana), right,
blooms brightest in May. Its sheltering mat often collects and germinates seeds of other plants.

Bunchberry dogwood (Cornus canadiensis) is a dwarf in a family of trees and shrubs. It grows only to about six inches, forming carpets in moist woods, especially west of the Divide.

Jones columbine (Aquilegia jonesii) is a plant of acute limits. It can grow only in limestone soils above treeline and is very rare.

Chipmunks, the smallest members of the squirrel family, are creatures of the day. Rarely do they appear before sunrise, and they retreat to nests or burrows before dark. Chipmunks are great collectors of food, both in cheek pouches and ground caches. They do not build up fat for winter hibernation and often wake to feed on stored seeds and berries. Three species of chipmunk are common in Glacier-Waterton, each adapted to life in a specific forest community.

North America's largest shorebird is the long-billed curlew (*Numenium americanus*); it is strictly an inhabitant of open country.

Few birds soar more gracefully on motionless wings than the white pelican (*Pelicanus erythrorhynchos*), a rare visitor in this region.

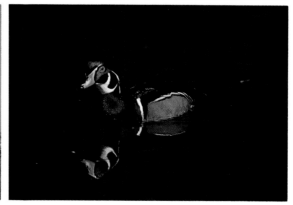

American avocets (*Recurvirostra americana*) nest in loose shoreline groups; they will dart at approaching predators noisily and en masse, trying to drive them away.

Wood ducks (*Aix sponsa*) lay their eggs in high tree hollows. When hatched, the young jump or tumble to the ground, unhurt by the drop, and toddle for home in the water.

A classic landscape of the Canadian Rockies, Moraine Lake, right, lies at 6,100 feet in the Valley of the Ten Peaks in Banff National Park, Alberta. The rock in the foreground is not a glacial moraine as geologists once thought (and as the name of the lake suggests); instead, it is the aftermath of a massive earthslide. The forest is Engelmann spruce and subalpine fir just as it often is at comparable heights 1,000 miles south in the American Rockies.

Early fall is truly the season of the elk (*Cervus canadensis*). Shortening daylight triggers hormone changes in both sexes, and the mating season, or "rut," begins. Large, prime, aggres-

sive bulls gather cows into harems, drive off younger competitors and breed. The woods echo with the bulls' challenge call, or "bugle," a loud, fluting, trumpeting, grunting sequence of notes as strange and haunting as any to be heard in the American wilds.

As late as the mid-1800s, large herds of elk
grazed the American prairie and meadows of
the eastern woods. Settlement has long since
pushed them from their native range, and now,
elk are almost entirely restricted to the wilderness country of the mountain West.

Avalanche Gorge (left) is in the deep forests on the west side of Glacier National Park. Meltwater from Sperry Glacier has carved this narrow slit through ancient red mudstones entirely since the end of the last Ice Age. Pebbles swirled round by rushing water sculpted the smooth, scooped out potholes.

Mule deer (Odocoileus hemionus), right, bucks move to the Glacier high country to summer in small bachelor groups. Their antlers, which drop and grow back each year, are covered by a soft skin, or velvet, laced with myriad blood vessels to nourish them. What evolutionary quirk has led deer to regrow whole new sets of antlers annually? Their function as both weapon and status symbol has dictated this. Broken points are replaced, and size appropriate to breeding vitality is added.

Smell is the "mulie's" keenest sense. While its hearing is sharp, and amplified by large ears, it cannot distinguish different sounds. But it can identify the scent of a man, or a mountain lion, or another deer in a whiff.

By early fall, a mule deer buck's antlers are full grown for the year. The velvet dries, peels and is rubbed off against trees. The coat grows heavier and turns from summer russet to winter gray. Hairs of this winter coat are air-filled for extra insulation.

52

Along the trail, a backpacker (right) pauses en route up the Cut Bank Valley in Glacier with Mt. Razoredge (8,560 feet) on the Great Divide in the distance. In the park alone, there are over seven hundred miles of hiking trail, traversing every life zone and all but the most severe terrain.

The roundleaved orchid (Orchis rotundiflora) blooms in mid-summer around wet, forested bogs in the Canadian north. Rarely does its range dip southward to the U.S.

Roots of the Rocky Mountain iris (Iris missouriensis) are deadly. Indians used a mix of ground iris root and gall on arrowheads; a mere scratch was said to kill.

Bright, nodding and abundant, blueflax (Linum lewisii) was another find of the Lewis and Clark journey. Its stem has tough, stringy fibers from which cord can be made.

A link in the chain, at the top of the pyramid: the red-tailed hawk is among the most common of its family. Crickets eat grass; frogs eat crickets; snakes eat frogs; hawks eat snakes. Hawks also die and are fed on by bacteria which breaks down their tissue which enriches the soil which grows new grass. This is the food chain, and no link is more vital than the other. The food pyramid gives another perspective on the natural world. At the base are green plants which are great in mass and number. Next come the plant eaters, everything from insects to mice to deer. Finally, at the top of the pyramid are the few predators: owls and hawks, weasels and mountain lions. It takes many acres of grassland at the base of the pyramid to support a single hawk at the top. Pave a meadow, and you'll kill a hawk.

Hawk food: these two ground squirrels—the golden mantled (Citellus lateralis), top, and the Columbian (C. columbianus), bottom—are both common in Glacier-Waterton where they are key links in the food chain. Both burrow under-

ground for safety, digging elaborate networks of tunnels and rooms. Both have also evolved eyes set toward the tops of their heads, giving them upward vision—and a better chance to see and flee the hawk as it drops from the sky.

*Come fall, bunchberry dogwood (Cornus can-
adiensis), left, are a good way to find ruffed
grouse. The mottled, chicken-sized birds feast
on these clustered red berries.*

*The black bear (Ursus americanus) has a
sharp nose, keen hearing and nearsighted
eyes. Some 75 percent of its diet is vegetable;
buds, bulbs, berries and nuts are all favorites.*

The largest of all grizzly bears (Ursus arctos) fed on the great prairie bison herds and followed them to extinction. Today, in the lower forty-eight states, the ''griz'' is limited to the vaster mountain wilds. About 200 remain in Glacier; smaller numbers also survive in the Bob Marshall and Great Bear Wilderness areas to the south. Grizzlies den for the winter with the first heavy, lasting snows, but they are not true hibernators and can be roused. By April, they are out and active again—feeding on roots, carrion, tubers, marmots, ground squirrels, deer, elk and moose as the warm months proceed.

The short-tailed weasel (Mustela ermina) is a voracious, streamlined carnivore that eats one-third its weight daily, mostly in rodents.

The nocturnal lynx (Lynx canadensis) preys on rabbits and hares when they're available; it prefers to still hunt rather than stalk.

The gray wolf (Canis lupus) is rare in Glacier and Waterton parks. Only between ten and twenty now remain; this is hardly enough for an effective, working pack.

When it can, the wolverine (Gulo gulo) will scavenge; otherwise, it will prey on whatever it comes across—anything from a porcupine, to a deer, to a young moose.

The clever coyote (Canis latrans) is more
thoroughly omnivorous than either man, bear
or pig. He will eat anything he can chew, not
necessarily digest, including, mice, rabbits, bee-

tles, watermelon rinds, crickets, berries, tire
rubber, bull snakes and green corn. His habi-
tats are equally diverse. Coyotes can work the
tundra, are at home in subalpine forests (right),
thrive on the prairie and are presently resident
within the city limits of Los Angeles.

Save for the great Canadian icefields, glaciers have finished their work in the northern Rockies—at least for this particular epoch. Today running water is the most active shaper of the Glacier-Waterton landscape. Where it flows from hard rock onto soft, it can create waterfalls. Where it flows through valleys, it may cut small gorges. Wherever it flows, it always works toward older bedrock, exposing signs of increasingly more ancient life such as the stromatolites, right, a fossil algae which dates back over a billion years.

Patches of white in the green woods: early morning frost on shoreline brush by a montane lake, and Indian-pipe (Monotropa uniflora), right. Indian-pipe is a curious plant, without chlorophyll and thus lacking photosynthesis. Instead, it is an attractive parasite, dependent on a special soil fungus of deep evergreen forests. This fungus, in turn, lives off the roots of green plants and serves as a "bridge" between the parasitic Indian-pipe and its true, food-producing host.

Sometimes it takes abrupt contrast to point up the diverse forms of life everywhere in process in the natural world. A pine and a mushroom are such a case. The ponderosa pine (Pinus ponderosa) seedling, left, is hard-

ly two inches tall while sinking a taproot two feet into the ground. Fully grown, it can stand over 125 feet tall with a trunk 24 inches across. The fresh "orange peels" (Aleuria aurantia), above, are tiny and pale in contrast to the three-inch size and dazzling brightness they will soon reach.

Aspen (Populus tremuloides) are literally the most colorful trees in the northern Rockies. In summer the leaves are rich green above and silvery beneath; both colors flicker into view as the leaves flutter in the wind. The bark is creamy white and seems to glow in the sun. Finally, in autumn, these abundant trees splash whole mountainsides with bright yellows, golds, oranges and sometimes even reds. The autumn display is triggered less by the first hard frost than by shortening daylight—a situation that also works with many animals including breeding elk (see page 44) and migrating birds.

The flicker (Colaptes auratus)
is a common woodpecker.
Adults swallow the food they
gather to feed their young;

when they return to the nest,
they regurgitate it into the
small birds' mouths with a
quick, pumping motion. The
young are never satisfied and
wheeze for more in response.

Old woodpecker holes and natural tree cavities are favorite nesting spots for the mountain bluebird (Sialia currucoides). The turquoise males do not help incubate the eggs, but once the young are born, they bring in a steady supply of insects for food.

The subalpine larch (Larix lyelli,) left, is an eccentric conifer that behaves like a leafy tree. In fall, its clustered green needles turn yellow and drop just as they do from an aspen or maple. The subalpine larch grows only near timberline, rarely reaching higher than thirty-five feet, but often becoming a strikingly delicate presence in the otherwise stark reality of snow, ice and rock.

Stamenate, or male cones of the lodgepole pine (Pinus contorta), release great amounts of pollen in June. This pine grows in dense, stockade-like stands. It is often among the first to return after a forest fire. This is because the female, seed-bearing cones resist heat, because the seeds grow well in ashy soil, and because young trees produce new cones when only ten years old.

Blue grouse (Dendragapus obscurus richardsonii), right, are also known as fool hens, for they are excessively tame. Encounter one along the trail, and sometimes it will just stand, stare and cluck—flying to refuge in a tree or hopping aside only to avoid being stepped on. Blue grouse nest from the low, ponderosa pine country almost to timberline.

When courting, male blue grouse, left, spread their tails, droop their wings, inflate their neck pouches and strut stiffly about. Their booming, hooting calls seem to echo through the woods from many different directions at once.

Avalanche Gorge in winter: the melt from Sperry Glacier has ceased, and only springs feed Avalanche Creek. Erosion by running water all but stops and ice takes over; the expanding and contracting of freeze and thaw chip off a sliver of rock here, force a crack there—all integral to the long, slow levelling that one day will reduce these mountains to an ultimate featureless plain.

Large mule deer bucks (Odocoileus hemionus) often summer along the scrubby interface between the alpine and subalpine zones. Rarely are they far from trees. The buck (above)—moving stiffly in alarm posture—is leaving the wide-open tundra for the safety of the spruce thickets below. Mule deer normally feed early in the day and again toward dusk. During midday, they bed down, right, choosing sites where they have a clear view of the surrounding land and where mountain updrafts bring them warning scents of any intruders.

HIGH COUNTRY

A mere 70 million years ago, the region of today's northern Rockies was awash with shallow, tepid seas. Then the ocean floor slowly began to lift at a rate measurable in no more than millimeters per year. For 100,000 centuries this uplift continued, though not always steadily, and by the time it ceased, the seas had been pushed far to the east and west, and a new mountain range was in place.

In the area of today's Glacier and Waterton parks, the uplift was accompanied by an oddity for here it raised the land on a tilt. Thousands of feet of old, stacked seabeds were heaved up and then, because of the tilt, a block 300 miles long cracked loose and slid, or overthrust, east for more than forty miles, again at a pitifully slow rate. The oldest of those seabeds exceeds a billion years in age, the fossils recording a time when algae was the apex of evolution. These seabeds, in particular, are the rock of Glacier-Waterton today. Ocean floor has become mountain top—in time.

It was a while yet, though, before the shaping would take place. Just three million years ago, the world climate cooled and North America plunged into the first of a sequence of Ice Ages which continues to this day. At least four of the deeper freezes were accompanied by massive glacial advances; during these intervals so much of the earth's moisture was locked in ice that the oceans dropped and a land bridge appeared across the Bering Sea between Siberia and Alaska. As glaciers commenced to carve U-shaped valleys and horn-shaped peaks from the northern Rockies, so ancestors of many of its animals migrated slowly across the land bridge—among them ancient elk, moose, deer, mountain goats and sheep.

The large glaciers retreated for the last time 8,000 years ago and by then the regional landscape was close to its present form. In Glacier and Waterton parks, the peaks, walls and valleys were like none other in the Rocky Mountain chain—primarily because the evenness of the ancient, overthrust seabeds allowed the glaciers to carve with an unimpeded, orderly grace.

Glacier and Waterton do not have the imposing mass of the Colorado Rockies; they lack the ragged power of Wyoming's Wind River and Teton ranges.

Here instead is an angular, sculpted quality that is unique. Peaks like Reynolds and Clements near Logan Pass and Wilbur above Swiftcurrent Lake, all in Glacier (see pages 77, 78 and 104), seem almost too fragile to be mountains—appearing more as improbably fine fins and rudders of stone.

If forms like these dominate the Glacier-Waterton skyline, the vertical aspect below and the regular U-shaped valleys further below are essential support. The landforms fit together; they have a symmetry, a coherent visible design that to most eyes is calming even in its grandeur.

The valley floors and midsections of the mountains are forested. However, as one moves upward beyond 6,500 feet in Glacier-Waterton, the trees shrink, become crooked and grow in scattered, sheltered islands. This is the high subalpine, and the further north one proceeds, the lower the height at which it begins. Altitude and the elements cause growth to cringe in self-defense; trees that are tall and straight down in the montane zone become hunched shrubs growing only in the protected lees of boulders and rims.

A few hundred feet above is timberline, and above that the alpine tundra, land above the trees. At first it's like being back on the prairie, for nothing has height except rock. Plants grow in cushions, mats and low clumps. The wind is hard. Save where marshes and streamlets leach from snowbanks and small glaciers, the tundra is dry. The mountain high country is a realm of sharp limits enforced by harsh conditions.

Light on the tundra is intense, five percent brighter than at sea level. Ultraviolet radiation has increased. Though there is ample rainfall at these heights, the incessant winds neutralize much of it. Water evaporates; snow is blown to valleys below; humidity down to ten percent is common. Temperatures are low; summers short; frost is possible any day of the year; soils are shallow.

The tundra is not a hospitable zone any more than the arctic north which it parallels. But there is a special clarity here that overrides other considerations. The geology is exposed and in order. Height and the experience of looking down give perspective. Life itself is purposeful and exact.

First-time explorers of the tundra are puzzled (and usually pleased as well) by the profusion of miniature plants. Why a sunflower full grown at six inches, a willow at two, and forget-me-nots in low mats? Small size is a universal alpine adaptation. It keeps life from the worst of the whipping winds. It means less exposed surface, cutting evaporation in the dry mountain air. Since survival of the species is foremost, it takes energy that might be used growing tall stalks and broad leaves and concentrates it on essentials: producing new seeds.

Other adaptations are equally apt. Many alpine plants cope with the short growing season by developing in stages: stems and leaves one year, buds the next, blossoms and seeds not until the third. Leaves are often covered by tiny hairs to diffuse the light and prevent burning. Low dense mats catch windblown dust to build soil.

Extreme conditions limit life's options and make its design more apparent. There are no lush, flamboyant gambles on the tundra. It is a world of precision, clarity and restraint.

An early summer stop along the subalpine trail: a blue backpacker's tent is dwarfed not only by the massive wall behind it, but even by the surrounding altitude-stunted spruce. Temperature at these heights, at this season, may reach comfortably toward the 80s by day, and dip to the chilly 20s by night.

Yearly rainfall in the northern Rockies, right, can reach one hundred inches, and the mountains let go of it slowly—from gradually melting glaciers and snowbanks and also from spongy, tiered marshes like those flanking Reynolds Creek near Logan Pass high in Glacier National Park. The process is more efficient and less costly than great big dams.

The white-tailed ptarmigan (Lagopus leucurus) is a compact alpine grouse. Chick mortality is about forty percent despite the superb protective coloring which makes them appear like lichen covered rocks or bundles of dried leaves. Hawks, eagles, coyotes and cold all take their toll. Only a third of each year's ptarmigan survive their first winter.

84

This small alpine marsh, left, near Logan Pass in Glacier is a center of dazzling mountain color. Lewis monkeyflowers, sedge and moss, below, dominate. Seen from above, the green of the surrounding, drier tundra seems almost

ashy in contrast. Source of such a marsh may be a glacier, a snowbank, a spring, or permafrost which holds the water constantly close to the surface. The marshy soils are dark, organically rich and often contain peat.

Krummholz! The word is German, means "elfin timber" or "crooked wood," and refers to conifers at timberline that have been twisted, gnarled and stunted by the severe alpine elements. This krummholz is subalpine fir (Abies lasiocarpa), a tree that often grows tall and straight to 75 feet in lower, more favorable climes. Here at 10,000 feet, however, it clings to a dense, shrubby life—hunched out of the desiccating wind in the lee of protecting rocks. Krummholz growth is pitifully slow; these trees are over ninety years old.

Lichens are primitive plants that evolved shortly after life emerged from the sea. They are the ultimate pioneers of the plant world, growing as easily on bare rock as raw sand. Acids from lichen break down rock, the first step in soil building. At high altitudes, lichens grow slowly, sometimes less than a half inch every thousand years! Pick up a rock crusted with lichen and hold antiquity in your hands.

Seasons in the high country can be disorienting. Sometimes summer doesn't arrive in warmth until July, followed by the onset of winter in August. Always, the first dustings of snow come early, whether it be on Mt. Amery (10,943 feet) in Banff, left, or along St. Mary Lake on Glacier's east slope, right.

Like their chicks, adult white-tailed ptarmigan (Lagopus leucurus) are masters of camouflage. From late spring to early fall on the tundra they are a mottled brown and melt into the land. Nesting hens are almost impossible to find. The sexes winter in separate flocks, and both turn snow-white except for black eyes and bill. Males gather in groups

of ten or twenty, remain above treeline through the worst cold and snow, and feed on tips and dried leaves of arctic willow. Ptarmigan will use primitive "snow caves," nestling down in the soft powder which blows around and over them, often covering them entirely. Snow insulates, helping protect ptarmigan from biting, wind-driven cold.

Rocky Mountain bighorn sheep (Ovis canadensis) have a complex, sensitive social system and from four to seven home ranges where they live seasonally. Lambs are born in late May on lambing grounds; after a week's seclusion, a ewe and her young rejoin a larger band where the arrival of the newborn can cause great excitement among barren ewes and subadults.

Young sheep are rarely alone. Females do not drive off their young after weaning or before giving birth to a new lamb. Young sheep learn their seasonal ranges from adults as traditions passed on from one generation to the next.

Bighorn ram's heavy, graceful horns have several purposes. They are both weapons (for butting) and shields, but most important, they function as symbols of dominance rank in ram bands.

Trophy hunting large-horned rams, right, may slowly decimate an entire sheep population. It can systematically wipe out genetically robust males just as they reach prime breeding stature.

After their second year, young bighorn rams voluntarily leave their mothers and join bachelor ram bands. By age 4½, they have inherited all this new group's seasonal home ranges. Loyalty to these ranges is strong; human disturbance is the most apt to disrupt these habits.

Bighorn's home ranges vary from a half mile to twenty miles apart. Usually at least one deep, timbered gorge separates these areas. Sheep migrate these distances at five distinct periods annually. If undisturbed, these journeys are measured and orderly, with the sheep following a leader single file.

In late November, bighorn ewes become ready to breed. Sheep society is organized so that dominant, large-horned rams do most of the breeding. The ram's courtship is cautious and is frequently interrupted by the intrusions of smaller, subordinate rams. Short, violent ram fights are common, but not harmful.

Parts of Grinnell Glacier, left, stretch along the Garden Wall in Glacier. When first studied in 1888, this ice river covered almost nine hundred acres; now it is down near three hundred, attesting to the cyclical cooling and warming of our climate.

For the hiker, two of the great pleasures of the alpine tundra are its openness and its dazzling, scattered splashes of color. However, freelance hiking here can be like walking heavily on a garden of glass. A single season's footfalls on a delicate tundra field can easily and unthinkingly destroy twenty or more years' slow, patient growth.

The gray jay (Perisoreus canadiensis), left, is notoriously known as the "camp robber," and the name is deserved. Many a wilderness traveler has had his unguarded bread, or bacon, or trout spirited away by this opportunist of the high forests. Gray jays are among the region's earliest nesters, often starting to work in February. Late snows can pile deep on the female's back as she sits and incubates the eggs.

The sticky shooting star (Dodecatheon cusickii) begins to bloom in the wet areas of the lower valleys in April and is still flowering in the high country in July. The higher it grows, the more compact its leaves and the shorter its stem. Late snows often catch the shooting star still in bud, but they do not deter its blooming.

Running water, plus hard rock, plus soft rock, plus height, equals waterfall. In Glacier, this combination of elements abounds. Swiftcurrent Creek has worked Redrock Falls from alternating hard and soft layers of the ancient Grinnell Formation. The lip of each drop is hard and erosion resistant; immediately below are softer layers through which this glacial melt has quickly cut.

Straddling the boundary of Banff and Jasper National parks, the Columbia Icefield is a massive token of what all this region was like some 10,000 years ago. Its dimensions are immense: ten miles by fifteen by over 2,000 feet deep. It

caps the Continental Divide and as lakes give rise to streams, so icefields are sources of glaciers. Three huge rivers of ice grind away from the Columbia Icefield; water melted from these flows eventually into the Arctic Ocean, Hudson's Bay and the Pacific.

If any one peak exemplifies the fine grace and sheer relief of Glacier's mountains, it is Reynolds (9,125 feet), left, astride the Great Divide at Logan Pass. Three massive glaciers, each moving independently, sculpted it to a classic, pyramid form before receding for the last time about 10,000 years ago.

The pika (Ochotona princeps) is a pint-sized alpine rabbit finely adapted to high altitude life. Short ears and legs, vestigial tail, chunky body and dense, insulating fur, all cut down on heat loss. Most unique, however, is the pika's crystalline urine which helps it combat the constant threat of dehydration in the dry, mountain air.

The heavily muscled Rocky Mountain goat (Oreamnos americanus) is a more skilled climber than the bighorn. Its hooves are convex and spongy on the bottom, giving the goat excellent traction to go along with a fine sense of balance. The rocky alpine slope above Many Glacier Hotel and Swiftcurrent Lake, right, in Glacier is mild goat habitat compared with the precipitous cliffs and narrow ledges they use for escape terrain and for bedding down at night.

Rocky Mountain goats have more varied food tastes than the bighorn, and they seem to do better in deep snow. The dark, dagger-like horns add a growth ring annually. Females use these for defense and males for combat as well. Goats do not butt each other frontally like big-

horns; most blows land on the rump and haunches where they may result in deadly wounds. Each spring, goats shed their dense winter coats, right, often leaving behind a trail of wool on rocks and brush—and also looking quite mangy for a spell. Never, however, do goats shed their beards.

Old rocks and new ice in Waterton Park create a vivid contrast between ancient and modern geology. The rock over which Cameron Falls (left) flows is Altyn limestone which may once have been a desert plain, a tidal flat, a delta or a plantless landscape we cannot imagine today. The mudstones of Red Rock Canyon (right) show billion-year-old suncracks, raindrop impressions and wave ripples.

*Winter quiet: October snows
settle over a heavily cankered
conifer in the Canadian Rockies. By February, these mountains and their forests are*

*transformed to a near mono-
chrome world of icy, glistening
white. This is the true depth
of winter in the northern
Rockies, and yet the first days
of melting are little more than
a month away.*

ALONG THE TRAIL
A Photographic Essay of Glacier National Park
and the Northern Rocky Mountains

was designed by David E. Spaw,
photocomposed in Palatino,
and printed on Warren's Flokote Enamel,
an acid-free paper with an expected
300-year library storage life as
determined by the Council of Library
Resources of the American Library Association,
by
The Lowell Press, Kansas City, Missouri